STORIES OF JESUS

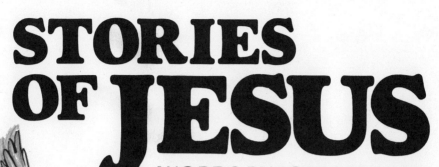

WORDS BY JOHN BEHNKE
OF THE PAULIST FATHERS
PICTURES BY BETSY ROOSEN
SHEPPARD

Paulist Press
New York, N. Y./Ramsey, N. J.

Library of Congress Catalog Card Number: 76-24440

ISBN: 0-8091-2063-1 (paper)
ISBN: 0-8091-0229-3 (cloth)

Published by Paulist Press
Editorial Office: 1865 Broadway, New York, N.Y. 10023
Business Office: 545 Island Road, Ramsey, N.J. 07446

Printed and bound in the United States of America

CONTENTS

Mary's Cousin Is Promised a Baby Boy — 6
Mary Is Asked To Be the Mother of Jesus — 8
Joseph Is Told That Mary Is Pregnant — 10
John the Baptist Is Born — 11
Jesus Is Born — 13
Shepherds Visit Jesus and Jesus Is Named — 14
Jesus Is Taken to Church — 15
A Messenger of God Tells Joseph How To
     Save Mary and Jesus — 16
The Three Wise Men Visit Jesus and His Parents — 18
Mary and Joseph Have the Scare of Their Lives — 22
John the Baptist Prepares the Way — 25
Baptism of Jesus — 28
Temptations — 30
Jesus Preaches for the First Time and Calls Two Disciples — 33
Jesus Goes to a Wedding with His Mother — 34
Beatitudes — 37
You Are the Light to the World — 38
Jesus Teaches Us the Our Father — 39
Possessions and Trusting in God — 40
Don't Judge Other People — 41
Jesus Helps an Army Officer — 42
Jesus Cures a Sick Man — 43
Jesus Does Something the People Do Not Like — 44
Jesus Helps a Man Who Can't Walk — 46

Jesus Becomes the Friend of a Sinner 47
Jesus Helps an Old Lady and a "Very Important Person" 48
Jesus Tells His Friends To Go Out and Preach 52
Don't Be Afraid To Say What You Have To Say,
    for God Is There To Help You 53
Following Christ Means Giving 54
Jesus Has a Serious Talk with His Friend Nicodemus 55
Jesus Tells a Story about a Young Boy
    Who Planted Some Seeds 56
Jesus Tells a Story about a Person Ruining
    His Next-Door Neighbor's Garden 59
Jesus Tells a Story About Some Boys Cleaning Up a Pond 60
John the Baptist Is Killed 62
Jesus Feeds a Big Crowd of People 65
Jesus Tells the People He Is Food Sent By God 66
Jesus and Peter Walk on Water 68
Jesus Does Some Teaching 70
Jesus Helps Cure a Very Sick Girl 71
A Woman with No Husband Gives What She Has 72
Jesus Helps a Widow Whose Son Just Died 75
The Greatest Rule of Them All 76
Jesus Visits His Friends Mary and Martha 78
Don't Always Be Thinking of Money 79
How To Act at a Party and Whom To Invite
    to Your Own Parties 80
The Story of the Son Who Left Home 83
Jesus Helps Ten People 86
How To Pray and How Not To Pray 88
Jesus and the Funny Little Short Man 90
Jesus Asks a Woman for a Drink of Water 92
The Woman Who Was Caught Sinning 94
Jesus Helps a Blind Man 96

Jesus Tells a Story 99

A Friend of Jesus Dies 102

Transfiguration: Jesus Shines as Bright as the Sun 104

Who's the Most Important Person? 105

A Story of How Happy God Is
When We Come Back to Him 106

How To Get a Person To Stop Doing Something Wrong 107

Jesus Hugs Some Little Children 108

Jesus Asks a Rich Young Man To Follow Him 110

Jesus Tells a Story About Some Workers Who Thought
They Weren't Being Paid Enough 112

Jesus Is in a Parade 114

Jesus Goes to the Temple and Becomes
Angry at What He Sees 117

Some People Try To Trick Jesus by Asking Him
a Very Hard Question 118

Jesus Tells a Story about a Rich Man and Three
People He Gave Money To 119

The Day God Will Separate the Good People
from the Bad People 120

Jesus Eats His Last Meal with His Friends 123

Jesus Prays in the Park and Is Arrested 126

Peter Follows While Jesus Is Taken to Court
and Sentenced To Die 130

They Nail Jesus to the Cross and He Dies 132

A Messenger of God Talks to Some Women
Who Visit Jesus' Grave 134

John and Peter Run to Jesus' Grave 135

Jesus Talks to His Friend Mary 136

Jesus Talks to Two of His Friends 138

Jesus Visits Peter and His Other Friends 140

Jesus Goes Back to His Father 143

Mary's Cousin
Is Promised a Baby Boy

A long long time ago there lived a holy priest. His name was Zechariah. He was married and his wife's name was Elizabeth. They didn't have any children. They had always hoped they would, but now they were both getting pretty old.

One day before he led the people in prayer, Zechariah was in the temple burning incense, and a messenger from God came to him and said, "Zech, don't be scared. God knows that you and Elizabeth have always wanted a child. God has decided that you can have your baby. He will make you both very happy. You'll be very proud of him. But one thing: you must call him John. He will be a great person. He will be the one who gets the people ready for when the Lord comes."

Zechariah listened to what the messenger had to say, but he really didn't believe him, so he said, "How can this be true? My wife is too old to have a baby." The messenger got mad at Zechariah and said, "I was sent by God to tell you this great news and you won't even believe me. Just for that, you will not be able to speak another word until your son is born."

Afterward, when Zechariah tried to lead the people in prayer, he couldn't say a word. All he could do is make gestures with his hands.

Later, when Zechariah had finished his duties in the temple, he went home. Elizabeth became pregnant just as the messenger said she would. She was so happy that she said a prayer to God. She said, "God, thank you so much. This has made me the happiest woman alive. You don't know how much I've wanted to become a mother . . . but actually you did, didn't you? Thank you so much. Amen."

Mary Is Asked
To Be the Mother of Jesus

One day a messenger was sent by God to ask Mary a question. The messenger's name was Gabriel. When Gabriel visited Mary, he said, "Mary, you should consider yourself very lucky. God is very pleased with what you are doing. He knows that you're a very holy woman." Mary thought that was a nice thing to say, but she was a little worried because she didn't know what Gabriel was getting at. Before she could say anything, Gabriel added: "Don't worry. Everything will be all right. God wants to know if you are willing to have a son and call him Jesus. He promises that this baby will one day grow up to be a great person. He will be a greater person than anyone else in the world."

Mary was very confused by all of this, so she said, "How can any of this happen? I'm not even married yet." Gabriel said, "God wants you to have this baby, so he's willing to perform a miracle. Your baby will be called the Son of God. I know it's asking a lot, but God really wants you to do it if you're willing. He doesn't want you to do anything against your will." Mary said to Gabriel, "I'll do it, but only if it's exactly the way you said it would be."

Joseph Is Told
That Mary Is Pregnant

You remember the story of how Jesus was born. God, the Holy Spirit, asked Mary if she would be the Mother of Jesus. She said: "Yes, I will." Well then, an angel appeared to Joseph while he was sleeping and told him the whole story. The angel said: "Joseph, Mary is going to have a baby. I want you to call him Jesus. He will be a very good and holy person. He is the one God has chosen to save the world. He will teach people how to live." This made Joseph very happy and he didn't worry after that.

John the Baptist Is Born

A few months later Elizabeth had her baby. It was a very healthy baby boy. She and Zechariah were very proud. Soon after he was born they decided to take him to the house of prayer for the ceremony in which they would give him his name. Some of the people who were going to go with them were very nosy. They said, "You're going to call him Zechariah, aren't you?" But John's mother said, "No, we've decided to call him John." John's father shook his head and agreed. He was so happy over the whole event that he started to pray out loud. He said, "God, I'm so happy that you have given me and my wife this beautiful baby. I have a feeling he is going to be a great person one day. I think he will lead many people to you."

John grew up to be a very good person. He loved God and lived a very simple but happy life.

Jesus Is Born

Now about that time the king wanted to find out how many people lived in his country, so he made the people go to their home towns where they were born and sign their names and the names of all the people in their families in a large book. This meant that Joseph and Mary had to make a long trip from Nazareth so that they could sign the book in Bethlehem.

Since Mary was pregnant and the time of Jesus' birth was near, the trip was a very hard one for her to make.

All the places where Joseph and Mary tried to stay were filled up, and there was no room for them. They had to take shelter in a shed where animals were kept. It was there that Jesus was born. Many people came to visit Mary and see the new baby Jesus.

And if you listened very closely that night, you could hear angels in heaven singing beautiful songs to God. One of the songs they sang was: "Glory to God in the highest and peace on earth to people of good will."

Shepherds
Visit Jesus
and Jesus Is Named

When the shepherds in that area heard the news that a baby had just been born in a nearby stable, they were very curious and went to see the baby and his mother. They found Jesus with Mary in the stable and were very pleased that Mary was feeling well and that Jesus was a healthy, normal baby. While they were there they said a prayer to God, thanking him because Mary and Jesus were happy and healthy. Later that week, when Mary was a little stronger, she took Jesus to the temple where he was given his name and welcomed as a member of the religious family. (This is the same thing that happened to all of us when we were baptized.)

14

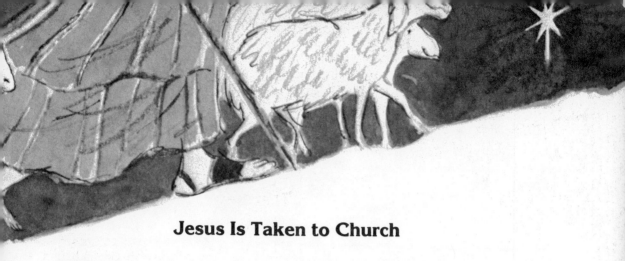

Jesus Is Taken to Church

When it was time for Mary and Joseph to take the baby Jesus to be blessed by the priest in the temple they took him to Jerusalem.

As they climbed the high steps and went into the temple, there was a very holy man inside who was praying to God. His name was Simeon. He was a very holy man and God had made him a promise that he would not die until he saw the person who was going to save the world from sin.

As soon as Mary and Joseph were inside, Simeon knew immediately that the baby in their arms was the one God had promised he would see.

Simeon ran over to Mary. He held the baby in his hands and prayed to God. He said, "God, now you can let me die if you want because you have kept your word. I have seen the person who is going to save the world from sin. I know that he will save all the people of the world, and so now I can die in peace. Thank you, God, for being so good."

Mary and Joseph didn't really understand all of Simeon's prayer. While they were trying to figure it out, other people came over to have a look at the little baby in Mary's arms. They all said very nice things about the baby.

After the temple ceremony, Mary and Joseph took the baby Jesus home.

The Three Wise Men
Visit Jesus and His Parents

After Jesus was born, many people came to visit him and his mother. One day three very special men came to see the newborn baby. They were astrologers and had been following the path of a star for many many days.

It wasn't an easy trip for them, and they had to ask directions many times. When they got close to where Jesus was born, they lost their way again and decided to ask the king of that land for directions. (The king's name was Herod and he was a very wicked man.) When they asked the king: "Where is this newborn king whom we have come to see?" Herod became very jealous and left the room. He called for his advisors and said, "What's this I hear about a new king being born around here? Find out who he is, because I'm the only one who's supposed to be a king in this country."

After looking in some old books the king's advisors reported back: "We found in some old books that the prophets said a king was supposed to be born in Bethlehem around this time. But that's all we could find out."

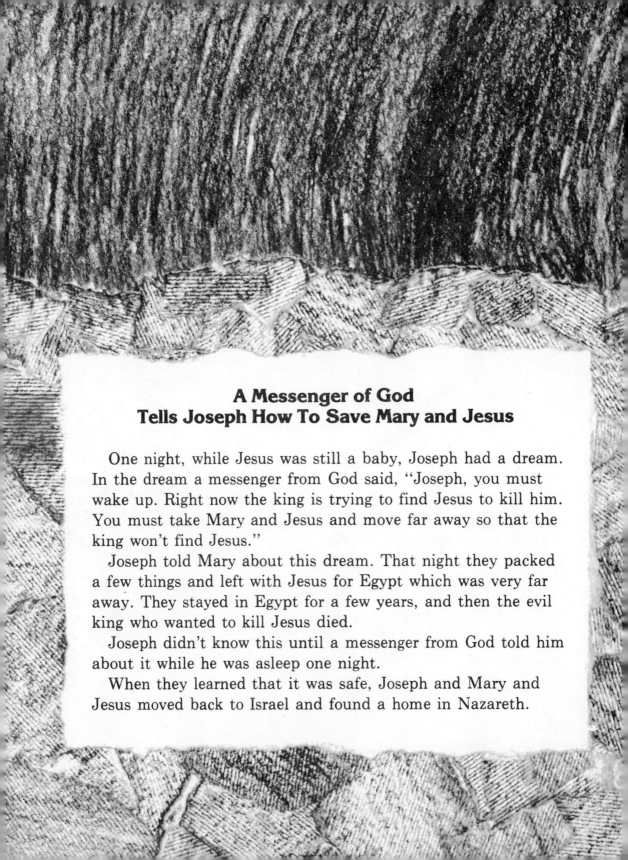

A Messenger of God
Tells Joseph How To Save Mary and Jesus

One night, while Jesus was still a baby, Joseph had a dream. In the dream a messenger from God said, "Joseph, you must wake up. Right now the king is trying to find Jesus to kill him. You must take Mary and Jesus and move far away so that the king won't find Jesus."

Joseph told Mary about this dream. That night they packed a few things and left with Jesus for Egypt which was very far away. They stayed in Egypt for a few years, and then the evil king who wanted to kill Jesus died.

Joseph didn't know this until a messenger from God told him about it while he was asleep one night.

When they learned that it was safe, Joseph and Mary and Jesus moved back to Israel and found a home in Nazareth.

Herod was still jealous and mad, and he said to the three astrologers: "My advisors tell me you can look somewhere around the town of Bethlehem. You should find the king you are looking for somewhere near there. On your way home, why don't you stop back here and tell me where this king is so that I too can go and visit and bring him a gift? And if you like, you can stay here and rest for a couple of days before you start out on your trip again."

The astrologers thought that this was a very kind offer and said: "Of course we'll do that on our way back home. It's very

nice of you to let us stay here." But it actually wasn't such a nice offer because all Herod wanted to know was where Jesus was so that he could have him killed.

The astrologers went on their way and found Jesus in the stable. They gave Jesus many beautiful gifts which they had brought from their own countries. They stayed quite a few days talking with Mary and Joseph. Then the night before they left they had a dream. In the dream they learned what Herod had in store for the baby Jesus, so the next day, instead of stopping by Herod's castle, they went home by another road.

Mary and Joseph
Have the Scare of Their Lives

Every year Joseph would take his little family to Jerusalem. They always went about the same time of the year so they could attend a very special temple service that only took place once a year. Nothing very unusual ever happened. Every year they would go and come back just like clockwork—except for one year when Jesus was about 12 years old. Mary and Joseph were almost scared to death. Everything went fine until it was time to leave Jerusalem to go home. Usually people from one town would travel in one group. The men would walk together and the women and children would walk together. Since Jesus was twelve and he was not walking with his mother, she figured he was old enough and must be walking with his father and the other men. And since Joseph knew he was not walking with the men, he figured Jesus must be walking home with his mother.

It was only after they had traveled a whole day that they realized Jesus was not with either of them. Very worried that something terrible must have happened, they hurried back to Jerusalem to look for him.

It took three days of looking all over town for him, but they finally found him. He was in the temple talking and listening to some of the most educated people in the whole country. They ran up to him and hugged him and said, "Jesus, we were so worried about you. We've looked all over for you. We thought something horrible had happened. Why did you do something like this? Why didn't you tell us?"

Jesus said something that his parents could not figure out.

He said, "Didn't you know that I must be about my Father's business?" They didn't understand what he meant but they were very glad that they had found him.

Jesus returned home—this time with his parents. He grew up to become a young man that any mother or father would be proud of.

John the Baptist Prepares the Way

One summer around the year 30 there was a man preaching to the people in the desert area near the city of Jerusalem. His name was John the Baptist. Actually he went all around the country telling the people he met that they should give up their sinful way of living and prepare for the coming of the Lord. In one of his famous talks about the coming of Jesus he said:

"Prepare the way for the coming of the Lord. Clear him a straight path. Every valley should be filled and every mountain and hill should be leveled. All the winding roads should be made straight and the rough and bumpy roads should be smoothed out so that the salvation of God can be seen by everyone."

(Actually we all know that he was really telling us to prepare our hearts for the coming of Jesus and not to fix the roads up.)

One day the people asked John the Baptist, "What should

we do to be good?" He told them, "If you really want to be good, you should share what you have with others. If you have two coats, give one away. If you have extra food, give that away too. If you are selling something, don't argue over the price. If you are a leader, then don't be a bully. Always tell the truth about someone. And be happy with the blessings God has given you."

As John was going around telling the people about the coming of Jesus a group of people didn't believe him. They said, "Who are you anyway? Are you some holy man? Are you one of those prophets we have been hearing about? Just who

are you that you think you have the right to go around the country saying those things to people?"

John replied: "I am simply a man who is telling all of you that the person God promised to send to save us from sin is coming very soon. We should all get ready by leading good lives. I'm no one very special myself. Actually I'm not even good enough myself to untie the shoes of the person God is sending. Be ready when he comes so you won't miss him."

After this meeting with these people John continued to tell people about Jesus' coming. He also baptized all the people who asked him to do so.

Baptism of Jesus

Jesus heard that John the Baptist was preaching near the Jordan River. It wasn't far away, so Jesus decided to go and listen to John talk.

At the end of his talk, John asked people to walk into the river and be baptized to show that they wanted to lead good lives.

Many people got up and went into the river to be baptized. Jesus went into the water too. When it was Jesus' turn, John said to him: "Jesus, I shouldn't baptize you. You should baptize me!" But Jesus said, "That's all right, John. I want you to baptize me." Right after Jesus was baptized, the people saw a beautiful dove flying around in the sky and they heard a voice that seemed to come out of nowhere say, "This is my Son. I love him very much."

Temptations

Just before Jesus started out on his preaching career, he decided that he had better take some time off and think and pray about it so that he would be sure he was making the right choice in his life. He decided it would be better if he got away from his family and friends and away from all the things that were going on in the city. He decided to go out in the desert to a place where he knew it would be quiet and nobody would bother him.

He spent 40 days praying and thinking. A couple of times he was tempted to just forget all about preaching and just go on doing what he wanted to. Even the devil tried to talk Jesus out of it.

The devil said to him, "If you are really the Son of God, take this stone I have in my hand and change it into bread."

Jesus was very hungry because he had been spending most of his time praying and thinking, but he said to the devil: "God gave me special powers to help other people. He does not want me to use my special talents only to help myself."

The devil didn't give up. He kept trying to tempt Jesus. He took Jesus up to a very high place where you could see for miles all around, and he said to Jesus, "I will make you the owner and ruler of all the land you can see if you will bow down and worship me."

Jesus answered: "That's a very tempting offer, but I can't accept it. You see, I don't worship anyone or anything but God alone." Although Jesus still hadn't given in, the devil was sure that he could find Jesus' weak spot, so he took him to the top of a tall building in Jerusalem and said: "If you're really the

Son of God, prove it to me. Throw yourself off this building. If you're really who you say you are, God will save you." Jesus said: "I cannot use my powers and talents just to prove that I have them. I must use them only to help other people."

The devil then gave up and went away, but that wasn't the last time he tempted Jesus. He came back many times during Jesus' life and tried to get him to do wrong.

Jesus Preaches
for the First Time
and Calls Two Disciples

Jesus went back to the city, but when he heard that John the Baptist had been arrested, he decided that it was about time to start his preaching career. After all, he had been preparing for a long time to preach. The subject for his first talk was: "Reform your lives. The Kingdom of God is near." He said, "The time has come. It's time to stop living bad lives. It's time to start doing what God wants you to do. It's time to start loving all people."

It could not have been easy for Jesus to get up and say those things because, just the week before, his friend John the Baptist had been arrested for saying the same thing.

It was a good talk. After he was finished, he took a walk on a beach to relax. He stopped to watch two men who were fishing from the shore. He said to them, "If you stop what you're doing and follow me, I'll make you fishers of men." Jesus talked to them some more, and it must have been the way he said things that made them decide to follow him. They left all of their fishing equipment right there on the beach. Later on that day Jesus convinced two other fishermen to follow him. They all became the best of friends. Their names were Peter, Andrew, James and John. They went with Jesus all over the country preaching the good news of love and helping people in need.

Jesus Goes
to a Wedding with His Mother

Shortly after Jesus met his first followers he was invited to a wedding in the town of Cana near his own home town. In those days, just as is true today, a party always followed the wedding, and Jesus attended it with his mother Mary.

However, before the party was over, all the wine had been used and there was none left for the guests. Mary knew that Jesus could do something about the situation, so she said to him, "They have no more wine." Jesus tried to explain to his mother that it was not yet time for him to show the power of God in him by performing miracles. But Mary knew that Jesus would help his friends and provide wine for them in order that the party could continue. So she said to those who were serving the food, "Do whatever he tells you to do."

Six jugs were standing in a nearby corner. Each of them held 20 or 30 gallons of liquid.

Jesus told them to fill the jugs with water. They filled them, and then Jesus said, "Now take some of the water out of the jugs, and bring it to the headwaiter to taste."

They were amazed because they saw that the water had been turned to wine. They did what Jesus asked and took it to the headwaiter. He was amazed, too, when he tasted the wine. He went to the bridegroom and said, "Other people usually serve the best wine first; and when the people have drunk a lot then they serve the poorer wine. But you have kept the good wine until last."

Beatitudes

One day, when Jesus saw that there was a large crowd of people who wanted to hear what he had to say, he climbed up the side of a hill so that they could all see and hear him. They all sat down on the ground and Jesus said:

"You're a very lucky person if you have learned to love just being alive. All the money in the world can't buy the best things in life.

"You're a very lucky person if you know how to be kind and understanding. People will want to be your friends if you help them.

"You're a very lucky person if you are always trying to make the world a better place in which to live. You will find that your life is very satisfying.

"You're a lucky person if you know how to be kind to other people, because they will be kind to you too.

"You're a lucky person if you stick to one or two things in your life and don't jump on every bandwagon that comes along.

"You're a lucky person if you work to have true peace throughout the whole world. You will be called a child of God.

"You're a lucky person if you can stand up for what you believe in. People will respect you and follow your example.

"You're a lucky person if you don't let it bother you when people pick on you and call you names because you believe what I tell you. If you can do this, your reward will be very great when you get to heaven."

You Are
the Light to the World

Jesus turned to his friends and said: "People look up to you.
They see how happy you all are with life. They want to follow
your lifestyle because they, too, want to be happy and at
peace. That's a very important thing you are doing. You can't
let these people down.

"You are a light to the world. Your life is an example for all
to see. It's like a city built on top of a hill. People can see it
for miles. You are like a light that someone puts in a room to
see with. The person doesn't hide the light in a closet. The
lamp is put on a table so it will be useful. That's what
happens to you too. You shine brightly out in the open so all
can see you and follow your good example."

Jesus
Teaches Us the Our Father

Jesus was talking to some people and he said, "Whenever you pray, don't just say a lot of words. You don't need to. God knows what you want to say before you start. Here's a prayer you should pray:

Our Father in heaven,
you are the holiest person there is.
May your Kingdom come
and your wishes be followed here on earth
just as they are in heaven.
Give us today our daily food.
Forgive us when we do wrong
just as we forgive those
who do wrong to us.
Don't put too many obstacles in our way
and keep us away from the devil."

Possessions and Trusting in God

Jesus said to his friends one day: "Don't worry about the small things in life. It's not worth worrying about what kind of food you're going to eat or what kind of clothes you're going to wear. Your life and what you do with it is much more important than what kind of food you're going to eat. Look at those birds flying around. God makes sure that they eat. Aren't you more important than they are? If God can take care of them, he will take care of your needs too. Look at those beautiful flowers over there. If God can clothe them with all those beautiful colors, then he will be able to take care of your needs too. Spend your time living good lives and God will take care of everything else."

Don't Judge Other People

One day Jesus said, "Let me tell you something that I have found to be a very good rule to follow. 'Don't judge other people and they won't judge you.' This is a good rule to follow because usually whatever you do to someone else they will do to you in return. Be careful that you aren't always going around finding little faults in everyone, especially since we all have big faults and someone might point them out to you. What you should do is spend time working on your own faults and not worry about the faults of other people. If you don't work on your own faults but go around telling everyone about their faults, then you're nothing but a hypocrite. And nobody wants to be called that."

Jesus Helps
an Army Officer

One day while Jesus was in a city called Capernaum an army officer recognized him. He walked up to Jesus and said, "I was wondering if you could help me. One of my workers is very sick. He can't move and he hurts all over. I've tried everything but there's nothing I can do for him." Jesus said, "Of course I'll help you. In fact, I'll come right now and see what I can do." The officer interrupted Jesus and said, "I know who you are. It's not necessary for you to waste your time coming to my house. If you just say the word, I know you can heal him right from here without even going near him."

Jesus was really surprised at the officer's answer. He said, "I've never had anyone put that much trust in me. All right, I won't go with you, and by the time you get home your worker will be all better." When the officer got home his worker was up and around. He was as healthy as he ever was before.

Jesus
Cures a Sick Man

One afternoon a man who had a very bad skin disease came to talk to Jesus. This skin disease was very contagious, so very few people would ever get very close to him. He said to Jesus, "Could you help me get rid of this disease? I've tried everything I know to get rid of it but it still stays." Jesus said, "Yes, I think I can. Let me touch you." Jesus touched the man on his cheek and all of a sudden the disease went away. Jesus told the man two things, "Go to the priest so that he can examine you to see if the disease is all gone. I'd like to ask you one other thing too. Don't tell anyone about this."

The man agreed to do what Jesus asked, but on his way to visit the priest he was so excited that he told everyone he met about his being cured. As a result all kinds of curiosity-seekers and people looking for a quick cure came to visit Jesus from all over.

Jesus
Does Something
the People Do Not Like

While Jesus was on his way to another city, two wild-eyed people jumped out of a cemetery. They had the devil in them. They started screaming at Jesus but what they were saying didn't make any sense. In a field nearby there was a herd of pigs eating. The demons in the men screamed to Jesus, "Command us to come out of these men and send us into those pigs over there." Jesus wanted to help the men, so he told the demons, "Go and live in those pigs, not these men." As soon as they did, the whole herd started to stampede. The pigs were so frightened that they jumped over a cliff and killed themselves. Needless to say, the people who owned the pigs were pretty mad at Jesus. They chased Jesus out of town.

Jesus Helps
a Man Who Can't Walk

One afternoon while Jesus was at home a lot of people came to hear him talk. The crowd was so big that they could not all fit in the house. Many of those who were outside stood by the windows trying to hear Jesus. Some people brought a man who couldn't walk to see if Jesus could cure him. There were so many people blocking the doorway that they couldn't get the sick man near Jesus. They were about ready to give up when they came up with an idea. They took the man up to the roof and removed the shingles over the room Jesus was talking in. When the hole was big enough for the man to fit in, they lowered him down on a rope.

Jesus felt very sorry for the man and all the trouble his friends went through, so he said, "Your sins are forgiven."

Some people who were listening to Jesus said to one another, "How has he got the nerve to say that? Only God can forgive sins." Jesus heard them talking to one another, so he said, "Why do you hate me so much? Let me ask you a question: What's easier—to say, "Your sins are forgiven," or to say, "Get up and walk"? While they were thinking of an answer, Jesus cured the man to show that he had God's permission to forgive sins. This whole event surprised everyone who was there.

Jesus Becomes
the Friend of a Sinner

One day Jesus was eating with his friend Matthew and some other people who were known to be sinners. Some very righteous people saw them all eating together and enjoying each other's company.

While they were watching the dinner party one of them said, "How can Jesus be eating with those people? Doesn't he know that they are all sinners? He even looks like he's enjoying himself." Jesus overheard what the man said, so he said loudly enough for everyone to hear, "People who are healthy don't usually go to see a doctor; sick people do. I have come to give meaning to those whose lives have no meaning. I have come to help the sinner."

Jesus Helps an Old Lady
and a "Very Important Person"

One day while Jesus was out on the lake in a boat a large group of people was waiting for him on the beach. As soon as he got out of the boat, the crowd gathered around him. A man named Jairus came up to Jesus and said, "Jesus, could you please help me? I'm very worried that my little girl will die. She's very sick. Please come with me and save her."

Jesus agreed to help, so they both started to walk to Jairus' house. While they were walking along an old sick woman began to follow the two of them. She was very sick. She had a sore that never healed. It kept bleeding.

She had gone to all the best doctors, but not one of them could cure her. She had heard about Jesus and was sure he

could help her, so she tried to catch up to Jesus as he walked along. As she walked along behind him, she thought to herself, "If I could only touch him, I'm sure I'd be cured. I wouldn't even have to talk to him."

Finally she was close enough and she reached out and touched him. Jesus felt someone touch him, so he turned around and said, "Who touched me?" There were a lot of people there, so it was hard to figure out who had touched him. When there was no answer, he asked the question again, "Who touched me?" Finally the woman admitted who she was and why she did it. Jesus said to her, "Your faith in me has cured you. Go and live a happy and healthy life."

After that Jesus and Jairus continued walking toward Jairus' home. Before they arrived some relatives met them and said, "It's no use. No one can help your daughter now. She died before you could get back home." Jesus turned to Jairus and said, "Don't worry. Trust me. Let's go to see your daughter." When they got to the house all the people were crying because the little girl had died, but Jesus said, "Don't cry. She's not dead. She's asleep." The people thought Jesus was crazy because they were positive she was dead.

Jesus, Jairus and his wife went into the girl's bedroom. Jesus said, "Little girl, get out of bed." The girl, who was only about 12, got up and started to walk around. The family was very happy that she was alive, and they thanked Jesus for coming and helping them.

Jesus
Tells His Friends
To Go Out and Preach

Jesus called his close friends together and said, "Now that you have been my friends for quite a while, there is something I want you all to do. I want you to preach the good news of God's love to people in different cities. I want you to try to help the people you meet who are sick. Up until now I have taught you all about the good news of love. Now I want you to spread this message to other people. Give it to whoever will listen to you."

His friends went out to nearby cities to preach after they got some last-minute instructions from Jesus. They did a lot of preaching and they visited people who were sick.

Don't Be Afraid To
Say What You Have To Say,
for God Is There To Help You

Jesus said to his friends, "When you go out to preach the good news of God's love, don't let people scare you. Just say whatever you have to. Don't be afraid of what people do to your body. They can't do any harm to your spirit. God will always be there to give you the help you need. To God you are worth more than all the gold in the world. If you're that important to him, surely he'll help you when you need it. So don't worry; let God do that."

Following Christ
Means Giving

Jesus said to his friends one day, "If you want to follow me, the going might get tough. It will not always be easy to constantly help other people. You might have to give up your whole family to become totally dedicated to my cause. But I promise you that I will never leave you stranded. In fact, whenever you give even a cup of water to a person who needs it, you will be giving it to me. The more you give to others, the closer I will be to you."

Jesus Has a Serious
Talk with His Friend Nicodemus

One day Jesus was talking to a V.I.P. whose name was Nicodemus. He said: "Nicodemus, God loves us and the whole world so much that he has sent his only Son to show everyone how to live. All those who listen to him and follow him will be happy living with God when they die. God didn't send his Son to earth to make life harder for everyone. He sent his Son to save us. It all seems very simple. God sent his Son to be an example for everyone to follow. He sent his Son to be a light to the world. Everybody who follows the light becomes a light for others. Those who sin all the time are not following the example of God's Son and so are not good examples for others to follow."

Jesus Tells a Story
about a Young Boy
Who Planted Some Seeds

One day Jesus was talking on the beach to a group of people. The crowd was so large that he decided to get into a boat and row out a few feet from the shore so that everyone could hear what he had to say. He told them this story. "One day in spring a young boy planted some seeds in a garden. When he sprinkled them on the ground a few birds flew down from a tree and ate some of them. Some of the ground in his garden was not good for planting because it was too rocky. The seeds started to grow in the rocky soil, but as soon as they grew a couple of inches tall, they died because when the sun was shining the rocks got too hot and killed all the roots of the plants. However a lot of the seeds were planted in very good soil and they grew to become very beautiful plants. The boy was able to pick more than enough vegetables to feed his entire family from the good plants." It was a very beautiful story and everyone enjoyed hearing Jesus tell it. Many of them, however, didn't know exactly what Jesus meant. Even some of his close friends didn't quite understand the story, so later on, when Jesus was just with his close friends, he said to them, "Don't you know that I really wasn't talking about a vegetable garden? I was talking about people who hear my message of love. Those who accept my message grow in love and spread it to other people. People who hear my message of love but don't accept it wither away on the branch and have nothing to give to other people."

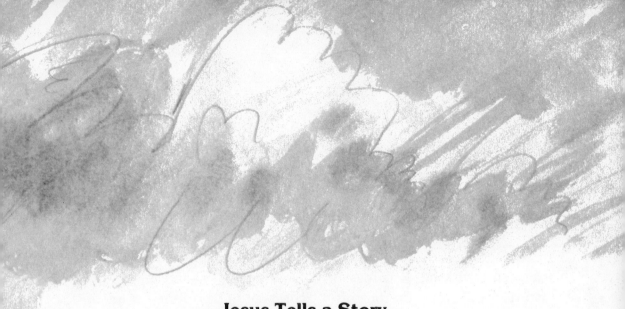

Jesus Tells a Story
about a Person Ruining
His Next-Door Neighbor's Garden

One day Jesus told his friends a story. He said: "One spring a man planted a small garden to help feed his family. He spent a lot of his spare time taking care of the garden. One night, however, one of his neighbors who didn't like the man threw the seeds from some weeds into the garden. When all the seeds started to grow, the man's son noticed that there were a lot of weeds growing in the garden. He mentioned it to his father and said, 'Dad, do you want me to pull all the weeds out of the garden?' The father said, 'No, you'd better leave them alone. Sometimes when you start pulling weeds out, a lot of the good plants get pulled out too. Let's wait till it's time to pick the vegetables. We'll pick all the vegetables we need and then we'll cut down the weeds and put them in the garbage.'" Jesus' friends really enjoyed the story but they didn't quite know what he was getting at, so he said, "The good seeds are those who listen to my message of love and spread it to other people in the world. The weeds are those people who are always making trouble in the world."

Jesus Tells a Story
About Some Boys Cleaning Up a Pond

One sunny afternoon Jesus was sitting on the beach talking to some people. He told them this story: "One day some boys decided to clean up a small pond in their neighborhood. People had thrown a lot of things in it. The boys got some rakes and started to scrape the bottom of the pool. They pulled a lot of junk out of the pond, but while they were putting the trash in the garbage bags they found a couple of dollars in loose change. They kept the money for themselves." The people listening really enjoyed this story. Then he said: "At the end of time, that is what God is going to do with all the people on earth. He is going to separate the bad people from the good people."

John the Baptist Is Killed

It seems that right around this time John the Baptist was getting himself into some trouble for telling the truth. He had the opportunity to meet the king one day. The king was living with Herodias, his brother's wife, and when John met him he said in front of everyone, "You know it's not right that you're living with your brother's wife." The king really got mad and had John thrown into jail. He wanted to have him killed, but he knew John had too many friends who could make trouble for the king, so he just let him rot in jail. Some time later the king was having his birthday party. He invited all kinds of important people to it. They all had a great time eating and drinking and dancing. As a special surprise Herodias' daughter

performed a special dance for all the guests. The king was so
pleased with her dance that he said, "That was the most
wonderful gift I could have received. I will grant you one wish.
Anything you want you can have. Just name it." The girl
wasn't sure what she should ask for, so she went to her wicked
mother for advice. When the mother told her what she should
say, she ran back to the king and in front of all the guests she
said in a loud voice, "I'd like you to give me the head of John
the Baptist on a silver platter." All the guests and the king were
shocked, but the king had made a promise and he didn't want
to lose face in front of all his guests, so he had one of the
guards kill John and bring his head to the girl.

Jesus Feeds
a Big Crowd of People

When Jesus heard that John the Baptist had been killed, he wanted to be by himself to think and pray. He went out to a very secluded place where he could be alone. Some sick people found out where he was and they went out to see him. Many people followed them. When Jesus saw how sick some of the people were, he felt sorry for them and cured them. It was getting late and all the people were still staying near Jesus. Some of his close friends said, "Jesus, why don't you tell these people to go home? It's getting dark and they're getting hungry. We don't have enough food to feed them all." Jesus said, "There's no need to act that way. How much food do we have?" One of his friends said, "Well, we have five loaves of bread and a couple of fish. That's not even enough to feed us!" Jesus said, "Bring me the food we have." He blessed the food that was brought to him, and then he said to his friends, "Pass out the food to everyone who is here." They did what he said, and when they had finished feeding everyone there was more food left than they had when they started. More than five thousand people had eaten. It certainly was a miracle to feed all those people.

Jesus Tells the
People He Is Food Sent By God

A couple of days after Jesus had fed the 5,000 people he went back across the lake to work. The people followed him again. When they saw him they said, "Jesus, we've been looking for you. Where have you been? When did you get here?" Jesus answered them, "You didn't come here to listen to me talk about God. You came because you thought you could get another free meal. You shouldn't be spending your time worrying about what you're going to feed your stomach with. You should be more worried about what you are going to feed your soul with." The people said, "If you want us to believe in what you say, show us a sign so we will know you come from God. Even Moses did that much for the people of his time. Come on! Show us a miracle!"

Jesus said, "It wasn't Moses who performed a miracle for the people. It was God who gave them that special bread from heaven. And even now it is God who gives you a special bread from heaven."

The people were confused because they didn't see any special bread, so they asked, "Where is this special bread? We don't see it."

Jesus replied, "Don't you realize I am that special bread. No one who comes to me will ever be hungry. I am the food of life sent by God. Anyone who eats this food will live forever because I am giving myself so that others may live."

Some of the people who were listening to him said, "That sounds like a terrible thing to say. Does he really mean what he's saying?"

Jesus said, "Yes. I'm serious about the whole thing. Unless you eat this food from God, you really won't have any life in you. Whoever eats this food will live forever in heaven. I was sent by God. I am living because of God. Anyone who eats this food sent by God will live forever too."

Jesus and Peter Walk on Water

One afternoon while Jesus and his friends were out for a boat ride, he asked them to drop him off on a nearby shore. He said to them, "I want to be alone for a while so I can do some praying. Why don't you catch some fish for supper?" Jesus lost track of the time while he was praying, and before long it was starting to get dark. He rushed down to the shore to call his friends onto the shore. For some reason, perhaps because it was getting dark out and the water was a little rough, Jesus' friends were a little frightened. When they saw Jesus they thought he

was a ghost. Jesus shouted out to them from the shore, "Get hold of yourselves. I'm Jesus. I'm not a ghost." Peter was still a little frightened, but he said, "If you are Jesus, tell me to walk on the water and come to you." Jesus said, "All right. Come on, Peter." Peter got out and began walking on the water toward shore. But then he realized what he was doing and became frightened. As he began to sink, he called out to Jesus, "Save me! I'm drowning!" Jesus pulled him out of the water and said, "You don't have much faith in me. Why don't you believe me when I tell you something?"

Jesus
Does Some Teaching

Some people who made believe they were leading good lives came up to Jesus with a complaint. They said, "We saw some of your friends eating without first washing the food really clean, as the rules say they should do."

Jesus knew that they just wanted to trick him and that they didn't always follow the rules, so he said, "A lot of people say they follow the rules, but when no one is looking they don't. I'm pretty sure you people don't always do what God has told us to do." Then he said to the crowd that had gathered, "It's not what comes from outside that counts. It's what you believe in your heart that counts. People who are very very bad are bad right to the core of their being. People who are very good are good right to the center of their hearts."

Jesus Helps
Cure a Very Sick Girl

While Jesus was preaching in a town, a woman from a nearby country interrupted him and said, "Jesus, have pity on me. My daughter is very sick. Will you cure her?" The friends of Jesus wanted to get rid of her because she was becoming a nuisance. Jesus said: "Tell me why I should help you. Your nation broke away from ours years ago and now you are our enemies." "I can't give you a really good reason," she replied, "but I do know that even dogs eat the scraps that fall from the table of their masters. Couldn't you just help me a little bit?" Jesus said to her, "You are very insistent, but your faith is very strong too. I will help your daughter to get better."

A Woman with No
Husband Gives What She Has

Jesus was talking to his friends one day about some things. He said, "Be careful of people who go around acting like big shots. Don't get fooled when people act as though they own the world and know everything. Most of these people are full of hot air. They'll take you for everything you have. If they ever do a good deed, they always do it when someone is watching them. It's all for show so that they will look good in front of other people."

Later on in the day Jesus and his friends were watching the people going into the temple. As they went in they would drop money in the collection box. There were some very rich people going into the temple and you could tell that they put a lot of money in the box.

Right after the rich people went into church Jesus said, "Look! Did you see that widow put some money in the box? She only had a couple of cents to throw in. But let me tell you —she really gave more than all those rich people did because they gave out of the money they had left over. This widow gave out of the money she had saved to buy food with. She has real faith in God."

Jesus Helps
a Widow Whose Son Just Died

Jesus and his friends had been in the town of Naim for just a few minutes when a funeral procession passed by them in the street. It was a very sad sight to see. The dead person was a young man. His mother walked behind him. She was a widow and she was crying very hard. Jesus felt very sorry for the woman. He stopped the funeral and walked over to the mother. He took her hand and said, "Don't cry." He walked over to the dead young man and touched him. Jesus said, "Get up." Immediately the young man sat up. Everyone was shocked. They had never seen anything like it before. They all were very happy, and they started thanking God for being so kind to the poor widow.

The Greatest Rule of Them All

One day a young lawyer came up to Jesus and said, "Jesus, what's the first of all the rules we have to follow?" Jesus said, "The first rule is: Love God with all your heart and all your mind and all your soul and all your strength. Love him with all you've got. And the second rule is: Love your neighbor as you love yourself."

The young lawyer wanted to do everything right, so he asked, "Who is my neighbor?" Jesus said, "Let me answer that by telling you a story. One day a man was walking down the road from Jerusalem. He was going to another city. As he was going around a bend in the road a couple of muggers jumped him from behind. They beat him up and robbed him of everything he had on him. They even took his clothes. They beat him up so badly that he was almost dead before the muggers left him lying in the road and ran away. Soon after an important religious leader was going down the same road. When he saw the man lying in the road he just walked around him and kept

going. He didn't want to get involved. It would have made him late. A little later another man walked by. He didn't want to be bothered either, so he just kept walking too. Finally a foreigner came down the road and when he saw the man in the road bleeding quite a bit from his injuries, he ran over to him and tried to help him. He finally got the bleeding to stop and then he brought him to a small boarding house and got a room for him so that he could rest for a couple of days. The foreigner had some business to take care of, so he paid the manager of the boarding house some money and asked him to look in on the wounded man until he was able to get back." Then Jesus said to the young lawyer, "Who do you think was a real neighbor in that story?" The lawyer said, "Why, the foreigner was the only neighbor to the man who was mugged." Jesus said, "Go and do the same thing yourself. Everyone is your neighbor."

Jesus Visits
His Friends Mary and Martha

One day Jesus went to visit a couple of friends of his. Their names were Mary and Martha. When they saw Jesus coming, Martha ran out and greeted Jesus in the front yard and invited him in. While Martha went into the kitchen to fix Jesus something to eat and drink, Mary sat down and started to talk to Jesus and listen to what he had to say. Martha got a little mad because Mary wasn't helping her with the work, so she said, "Jesus, I'm out here doing all the work. Will you tell Mary to come out here and help me? There's an awful lot that has to be done!" Jesus said to Martha, "Martha, don't get so upset. Relax a little. You don't always have to be running around fussing over little things. Mary and I are having a nice conversation. Among friends that's more important than having some refreshments. Why don't you come out and join us?"

Don't Always
Be Thinking of Money

On a sunny afternoon while Jesus was talking to a group of
people, one of the men said, "Jesus, I've got a problem. Will
you make my brother give me my share of the money that was
left to both of us? He won't give me a cent." Jesus said, "I'm
not a judge. I can't do that. Besides, people shouldn't be so
greedy. Money isn't the most important thing in life. Let me
tell you a story. There once was an old miser who had so much
money he didn't know what to do with it all. His safes were
not enough to hold all the money. So he had his workers build
bigger and better ones to put his money in. Then he thought to
himself, 'Now I don't have to worry. I've got all the money I'll
ever need for the rest of my life. I can sit back and enjoy life.'
But that night the old miser died in his sleep. He never got to
use any of the money. It wasn't any good to him. That's what
happens when a person only thinks about himself."

How To Act at a Party
and Whom To Invite
to Your Own Parties

One weekend Jesus was invited to a dinner party. When he got there he noticed how everyone was trying to sit in the best places at the table. So he told this story to them: "As you know, when you go to a wedding party you always try to be on your best behavior. You don't run to the dinner table and take the best seat, for you might be embarrassed when the host comes up to you and asks you to sit somewhere else because the seat you've taken is for a V.I.P. That's awfully embarrassing! What you should do is always take the least important seat so that the host will come up to you and say, 'What are you sitting here for? You should be at the head table with the other important guests.' Then you won't be embarrassed, but you'll be honored. Anyone who thinks he's important and acts that way really isn't."

Then he went on to say, "When you have a party, don't just invite friends and relatives who you know will invite you back to their parties. Ask some people who probably never get out to a really nice party. Ask some people who can't invite you to a party because they can't afford to have one. If you do this you may not be rewarded here, but you certainly will be when you die and go to heaven."

The Story of the Son Who Left Home

Once upon a time there was a man who had two sons. One day the younger son said to his father, "Father, give me right now the money you intend to leave me when you die." The father consented. Then the son, as soon as he had his money, left home and went far away without even bothering to send any news. There he began to squander all that he had received. At that time a terrible famine came over the country. No one came to his help, so he got work on a farm. His job was to take care of the pigs. He would have liked to eat the food that the pigs were eating, but he was not allowed to do so. Pretty soon he didn't have a cent to his name. He was really starving when he began thinking about his own country. He said to himself, "My father's workers have plenty to eat. I'll go back home and say to my father, 'Father, I have sinned against you. I am no longer worthy to be called your son. But please take me back anyway, as one of your workmen.'" So he set out on the road home. When he was still far off, his father saw him coming. Beside himself with joy, he ran to meet his son, threw his arms around him, and kissed him. The son began to say, "Father, I have sinned against God and you. I am no longer worthy to be called your son." But his father interrupted him, turned to his servants, and said, "Quickly now, bring out the finest robes, and prepare a big feast. This is a great day, because I have found my son whom I believed to be lost."

While all this was going on the older son was out working in the fields. On his way back home after work, he heard music and a lot of laughter. He called to one of his servants and asked "Hey, what's going on?"

The servant said, "Your younger brother came home unexpectedly and your father was so happy he decided to have a party to celebrate."

The older brother got very angry and refused to go to the party. His father saw what was happening and tried to get him to stop pouting and come to the party. The older son, still

feeling hurt, said, "Dad, this really burns me up. For years I've been doing everything you've wanted and have helped you all I could. But you never once threw a party for me. Now my young brother who has done nothing right all his life, and who has hurt you everytime he turns around, has a big party in your house. And to top that off you're giving the party. It's just not fair!"

The father said, "Look, son, you have always been with me and I love you very much. You know that. Everything I have will one day be yours. But I just had to have this party for your brother. I thought he was dead, but he's really alive and has come back to us. This makes me very happy. I hope you can understand that."

Jesus Helps Ten People

On a trip one day to the city of Jerusalem, ten men with a very contagious disease came up to Jesus. They didn't get too near to him but close enough for Jesus to hear what they had to say. They said to him, "Jesus, help us. We really are sick and you're the only one who can help us. If you don't help us, we'll die." Jesus said, "I'll help you, but first go and show yourself to your priest." (In those days priests were supposed to check over people who had that kind of disease.) As they went to see the priest something very strange happened to all ten of them. They were all cured! They were so happy that they all started to jump for joy. One of them decided to go back and thank Jesus for what he had done. This man was a little different than the others because he was actually a foreigner. When he found Jesus he couldn't stop thanking him. Jesus was very happy to see the man all better, but he was also a little hurt. He said to the man, "Didn't I help ten of you? Where are the other nine? Didn't they have the decency to come back and thank me too?" Then Jesus said to the foreigner: "Your kindness and faith are very great. You will be a very good person."

How To Pray
and How Not To Pray

On an ordinary day, pretty much like today, Jesus was talking to a small group of people who thought an awful lot of themselves. In fact, they really thought they were better than most of the people they knew. Jesus wanted to point out to them that they were a little too stuck up, so he told them this story. He said, "Once upon a time, two men went to the temple to pray. One of them was a V.I.P. The other one was a tax collector (not too many people liked him). The V.I.P. went up in front of the temple and started praying. He said, "God, thanks for not making me like the rest of the people. I'm pretty good and I know it. I'm not like that tax collector over there. I'm glad you made me better than other people." (That was some prayer.) The tax collector didn't stand so close to the altar when he prayed. He kept his eyes down and said in a very low voice, "Please, God, help me. I know I'm a sinner. I know I've done some bad things in my life. I'm not perfect. I need your help to be a better person."

Then Jesus said, "The tax collector is the better person of those two because he wasn't always claiming to be better than anyone else. He was the really honest and good person."

Jesus and the
Funny Little Short Man

One day toward evening Jesus was walking through the city
of Jericho. There was a big crowd of people standing all around
Jesus, so it was really hard to see him. In the crowd trying to
see and hear Jesus was a funny looking little short man named
Zacchaeus. He couldn't see Jesus so he decided to climb a
nearby tree. Then he would be able to look down on Jesus.
When he had been in the tree for a few minutes, Jesus looked
up and noticed him. He said, "Zacchaeus, come down out of
that tree. I'd like to stay at your house tonight." He came
down and the people let him get near Jesus. But some of the
people muttered, "How could Jesus stay with that man? He's a
sinner!" Zacchaeus heard them whispering, and he said to
Jesus, "I know I've done some bad things in my life, but now I
want to make up for all those bad things. I'm going to give half
of all I have to the poor. And if I have ever cheated anyone I
will pay that person back four times the amount I took." Jesus
was very pleased with what Zacchaeus had said, and so he
said, "Today you have been saved because you have changed
your life from doing evil things to doing good things. What was
lost has been saved."

Jesus Asks
a Woman for a Drink of Water

One day while Jesus was walking, he became very tired. He sat down by a well to rest for a while. He was thirsty too because it was very hot out, but he didn't have anything with which he could pull the water out of the well. Finally, after a long wait, a woman came by to get water for her home. When Jesus saw her coming he jumped up and asked, "Will you give me a drink of water, please?" (Back in those days there were a lot of class distinctions and normally no one would ask that woman for anything. So naturally the woman was surprised by Jesus' question.) She said, "Sir, no one like you has ever asked me for anything." Jesus surprised her again by answering: "If you knew who I was, you would ask me to give you living water

so that you would never thirst again." She said, "You sound like you're pretty important. Who are you—a prophet?" Jesus then told her things about herself which only she and God could have known, so she believed that Jesus was a very holy person. He then explained to her what he meant when he said he was the living water, and he talked to her about doing good for other people and loving all people.

When she went home she led many other people to believe in Jesus and live good lives.

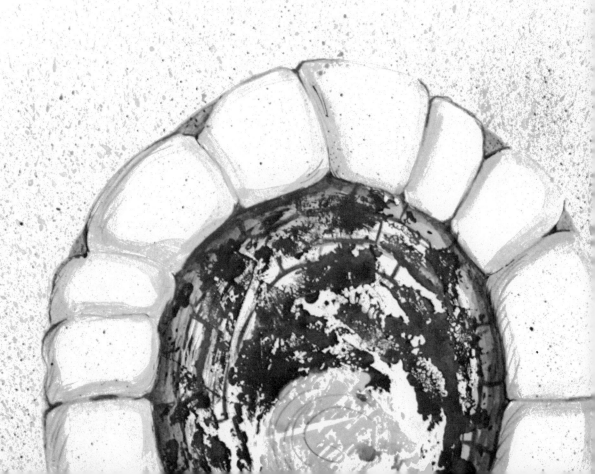

The Woman
Who Was Caught Sinning

One day while Jesus was talking to a group of people about
some important matters a group of leading citizens broke into
the conversation. They threw a woman down at the feet of
Jesus. She looked as though she had been beaten up. They said
to Jesus, "This rotten woman has been caught by us
committing a very bad sin. The law says she should be killed.
Do you want to help us?" Their pushy attitude made Jesus
mad but he didn't say a word. He bent down and started
doodling with his finger on the ground. Then he looked up and
said, "Let whichever one of you has never sinned in his
life throw the first rock to kill this woman." Embarrassed by
what Christ had just said, they started to leave one by one.
Finally the only two people left were Jesus and the woman.
Jesus looked kindly at the woman and said, "You can go now.
I will not hurt you. But try not to sin anymore."

Jesus Helps a Blind Man

One day while Jesus was walking through the streets of a city, he beheld a very sad sight. He saw a young blind man begging for food. From looking at him it was obvious that he had been born blind.

Some people walking with Jesus asked: "Why is this man blind? Is it because his parents committed a serious sin, or did he himself do something bad? Is that why God is punishing him?"

Jesus was amazed at these questions and answered: "How could you even think that? God loves us. He doesn't punish people that way for committing sins. This man or his parents may never have committed a serious sin in their lives. You shouldn't judge people to be bad just because they look different from us."

Then Jesus said something else which startled all of them. He looked them squarely in the eyes and said: "I am the light of the world." Bending down to the ground he mixed some saliva and dirt in his hand and made mud out of it. Then he smeared the mud all over the man's eyes. "Go and wash that mud off," Jesus said to the blind man. When the blind man washed his face he couldn't hold back his excitement because for the first time in his life he was able to see.

Then Jesus said to the people: "I was sent into this world to make people see not only with their eyes but also with their hearts. I have come to help people see how to live good lives."

Jesus Tells a Story

One day Jesus was trying to make an important point with his friends. He gave them a few examples to make what he was saying a little clearer.

Jesus said, "Have you ever noticed that when a father comes home from work, he uses his key to unlock the door and comes in the front door and shouts to his wife and kids, 'Hi, I'm home'? The family runs to him and kisses him because they are happy to have him home. He spends the whole day working so that the family will have enough food to eat and enough clothes to wear. He comes home at night to love his family and to protect them and sometimes to help them with homework. If necessary, a father would even die to help his family. The family loves to have their father home.

"Have you ever heard stories about a thief who breaks into a house by climbing in a back window? If the people are home, he almost scares them to death. Sometimes a burglar will beat up the people and lock them in the closet. All he is interested in is stealing money and valuable goods. It's very scary and frightening to have a robber in your home."

Jesus then said to his friends, "I am like the father who loves his family. There is nothing a good father wouldn't do for his family. I want you to know that there is nothing that I wouldn't do for you because I love you all very much. You should try to be that way too.

"Have you ever known anyone who owned a bunch of dogs? I

did. This man really loved his dogs. He took care of them. He fed them. He took them for walks every day. He even gave them baths when they needed one. They were very happy dogs and the man loved them very much. This man loved those dogs so much that he would rather die than let someone hurt his dogs. This man never let anyone else take care of the dogs because he knew that they did not love the dogs as much as he did and so they wouldn't get as good care.

"There's a good lesson there for all of us. I try to be like that man even with my friends. I try to love them and help them and make them happy. There's nothing I wouldn't do for a friend. I'd even give my life for a friend."

A Friend of Jesus Dies

Jesus was preaching to some people when he received a note from his friends Mary and Martha. The note said, "Dear Jesus, our brother Lazarus is very sick. We think he is going to die. Can you come quickly? We need you. Love, Mary and Martha."

Jesus was a long distance away. Before he got to their home Lazarus had died. In fact, when Jesus did finally get there Lazarus had been buried for four days. Everybody was very upset because Lazarus had died so quickly and so unexpectedly. Mary and Martha hadn't eaten or slept for days. When they saw Jesus they both ran into his arms and began to cry. They both were very upset. "Jesus," they said, "if you only could have gotten here sooner, maybe all of this wouldn't have happened." Jesus said, "Don't worry. Your brother will come to life again! I am the source of life. Anyone who believes in me will always have life." Jesus began to cry too because he felt very badly that Lazarus had died before he got there.

Then he said to them, "Will you take me to the tomb where you buried him?"

When they got there Jesus said, "Move the stone away from the doorway of the tomb."

Jesus prayed to his Father in heaven and shouted into the tomb, "Lazarus, get up and come out here."

A few moments later Lazarus came out of the tomb. None of those present could believe their eyes. All the people began to cry because they were so happy to have Lazarus back with them. And that night they had a wonderful party to celebrate.

Transfiguration:
Jesus Shines as Bright as the Sun

One day, Jesus and three of his close friends went up on a mountain to pray together. Jesus' friends, Peter, James and John, were very tired and they fell asleep. So Jesus prayed by himself. While he was praying, he had a vision and talked to two saints from the Bible stories. Their names were Moses and Elijah. While Jesus was talking to these famous people, Peter woke up and saw what was going on. Peter heard a voice coming out of the sky saying, "This is my Son: listen to him." After the vision went away, Peter said, "Jesus, this must be a very holy place because you were talking to the saints right here. Let's build a place of worship on this spot so that other people can come and pray here too." But Jesus told Peter that it was not the right time to tell the world about what had happened, and so they decided not to build the place of worship.

Who's the
Most Important Person?

One day on the way home Jesus heard his friends discussing something. He said, "What are you talking about?" None of them wanted to tell Jesus because they knew he wouldn't like it. Finally one of them said, "We were just trying to decide who was the most important." Jesus said, "Let's sit down and talk about it." They sat in a circle and then Jesus said, "Don't you know that if you really want to be first in God's eyes, you have to serve the people around you.

"You really should accept everyone as equals. No one's more important than another person. Even a child like this one sitting here is important. You should be as kind to her as you are to me."

A Story of How Happy
God Is When We Come Back to Him

One morning while Jesus was talking to his friends he said, "Do any of you know a cat-lady? I do. She has so many cats you couldn't count them all. But she knows every cat. Each one has a name she gave it. She is very careful with them. She doesn't let them get out of the house. But every once in a while one gets out and gets lost. Whenever that happens she gets worried sick. She spends all her time roaming up and down the streets and alleys till she finds the lost cat. She won't rest until she finds the cat and brings it home safe to her home. That's the same way it is in heaven when someone who is always sinning on earth stops. There is a lot of rejoicing that goes on."

How To Get a Person
To Stop Doing Something Wrong

Jesus said to his friends, "Let me tell you what to do if you find out that a friend of yours is doing something wrong. Take the person aside where no one will hear the two of you talking and ask your friend, 'Do you know what you are doing?' Try to get your friend to stop doing wrong. If that doesn't work, ask another friend or two to come with you to talk things over together. If that doesn't work, get a priest to talk to your friend. If that doesn't work, then you have done all that you can. The only thing left is to pray for your friend."

Jesus Hugs
Some Little Children

Later on that day a lot of parents were bringing their children to Jesus so he could bless them. There were an awful lot of children around and it got pretty noisy. Some of Jesus' friends who were older didn't like all the noise and running around, so they tried to chase the parents and children away. Jesus was really surprised at what his friends were doing, so he said, "Let those children alone. Just look at them. They're so innocent. Aren't children beautiful? I wish everyone could act just as they do. In fact, if we grown-ups aren't as accepting and as good as these little children, we'll never get into heaven." Then Jesus took a couple of the children in his arms and gave them both big hugs.

Jesus Asks
a Rich Young Man To Follow Him

One day Jesus was getting ready to go on a trip. While he was packing a young man came up to him and said, "Jesus, what must I do to be able to live with God in heaven?" Jesus answered, "You look like an intelligent young man. I'm sure you know what the rules God gave us are. Don't kill. Don't steal. Don't lie. Love your parents."

The young man said, "Yes, I know all that, and I follow all those rules. But I want to do more." Jesus said, "Well there is one other thing you could do. You could sell everything you have. Give the money to the poor and then come, follow me." This answer surprised the young man. He didn't know if he wanted to do that because he was very rich and he had everything he ever wanted. He left Jesus very sad and never returned.

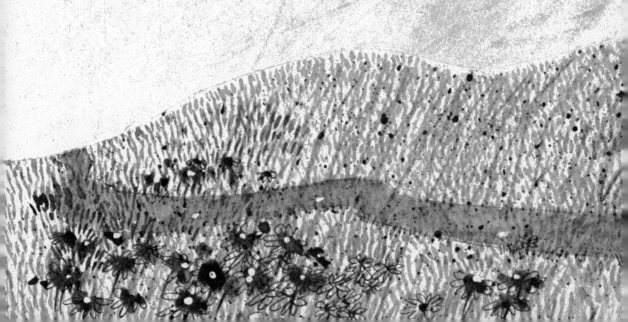

When he was gone Jesus said, "It's very hard for rich people who have everything to follow what God wants them to do because they can buy their way in and out of anything they want. Let me say this, though. Anyone who gives up a lot, like a home and parents and friends, to follow me will be rewarded one hundred times more than what he or she gave up."

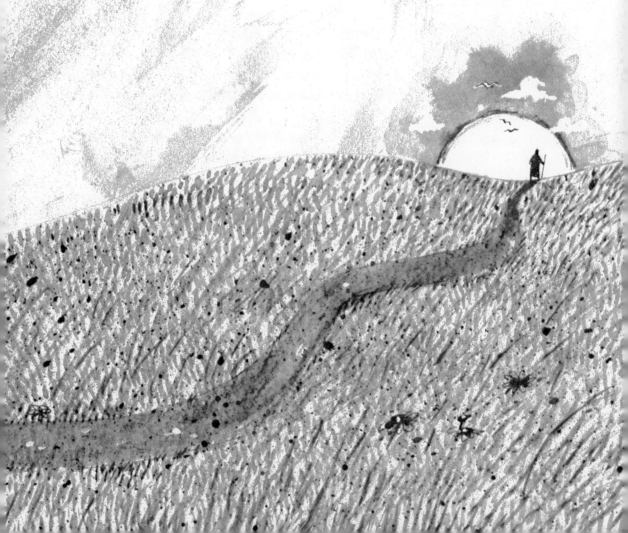

Jesus Tells a Story About Some Workers Who Thought They Weren't Being Paid Enough

Jesus wanted to tell his friends a good story, so he had them all sit down and get comfortable. Then he said, "Once there was a man who owned a big farm outside of town. There were many people who worked for him all the time, but when the work got behind he used to hire more people just for the day or for a couple of hours. One day he had to hire some extra people because there were too many tomatoes for his regular crew to pick. He needed about ten extra people, so he went to the unemployment office to hire them. When he got there, he found only three people who needed a job. He said to them, 'I'll pay you $25 if you put in a good day's work.' Then he told the employment agency, 'I'll be back at noon to see if anyone else needs a job.' He came back alone at noon and there were seven more people who were looking for jobs. Seven was just

the right number he needed, so he hired them all. He put them to work for the afternoon. When the work for the day was done, the man gave each of the ten people he had just hired $25. The first three people started to complain to the man: 'How come these people only worked half the time we did and are getting paid the same as we are?' The man said, 'I don't have to answer your question but I will. Didn't we agree that I would pay you $25 for your day's work? Why are you angry because I have been generous with these other people? You three get out of here. I'll never hire you again for anything!'" When Jesus finished the story he said to his friends, "Do you know what the moral of this story is? Never be jealous over the good fortune of another person. You should be very happy for that person."

Jesus Is in a Parade

When Jesus arrived near the city of Jerusalem, his disciples found one of the best riding animals in the area. They borrowed it and made a saddle out of their coats. They helped Jesus get on the top of the animal and then had a parade into the city streets of Jerusalem. It was a marvelous parade.

As Jesus passed by, the people threw tree branches and flowers down on the road. They waved at Jesus with their hands, with colorful pieces of cloth, and with palm branches which they had cut down from nearby trees. After he passed they joined in the parade itself. They sang many happy songs.

Jesus Goes to
the Temple
and Becomes Angry at What He Sees

A couple of days before a big religious celebration Jesus went to Jerusalem. That afternoon he decided to go to the temple to say some prayers. When he got there he looked at the outside of the beautiful temple and then went in. As he looked around inside he couldn't believe his eyes. There were lots of people there but nobody was praying to God. Some of them were selling things, others were buying souvenirs, and still others were just panhandling. Jesus got so mad at what he saw that he started shouting: "Get out of here! What do you people think you're doing anyhow? This isn't just some sidewalk where you can do anything you want. This is the house of God." At this point he was so mad that he started pushing their tables over, and he didn't stop until they all got out of the temple.

As the people were running out of the temple someone shouted out to Jesus, "What gives you the right to do this to us? Prove to us that you have the right!"

Jesus said something very unusual at that point. He said, "Keep destroying this temple as you have and I will rebuild it in three days." The people didn't understand what he was talking about because the temple originally took about 50 years to build. But they were in such a hurry to get out of there that they didn't stop to ask Jesus what he meant. (But now we know that Jesus was actually talking about his death and resurrection and not just rebuilding an old temple.)

117

Some People Try To Trick Jesus
by Asking Him
a Very Hard Question

The temple officials were always trying to get something on Jesus, so whenever they saw him they would ask tricky questions. However, Jesus was always able to beat them at their own game. One day these officials said to Jesus, "You are a very good man. We respect your opinion. Is it right for us to pay our taxes to the king?" Jesus knew what they were trying to do, so he said, "Why are you always trying to trick me? You're nothing but a bunch of hypocrites, but I'll answer your question. Whose face is on the front of the money we use?" They said to him, "The king's." Jesus replied: "Give to the king what is the king's and give to God what is God's!"

Jesus Tells a Story about a Rich Man and Three People He Gave Money To

One night when Jesus was together with some of his friends he told them this story: "Once upon a time a rich man was going on a long trip. He called three of the people who worked for him into his office. He said, 'I'm going away for a couple of months. While I'm gone I'd like each of you to invest some money for me. See how much money you can make with what I give you!' He did this as a test because he wanted to promote these people to better jobs. Two out of the three people doubled the money they were given. The third person just put the money in a drawer and didn't even try to make any money. When the man came back after two months he promoted the first two people, but he fired the one who didn't do anything."

The Day God Will Separate
the Good People
from the Bad People

One sunny afternoon Jesus said to his friends, "At the end of time God will come to judge everyone who ever lived on earth. He will separate the people into two groups. All the good people he will put in one group. All the people who led bad lives he will put in another group. He will say to the good people, 'Come! I have prepared a wonderful place for you all. When I was hungry you fed me. When I was thirsty you gave me a drink. When I was a stranger you welcomed me into your homes. When I was sick you took care of me. When I was in prison you came to visit me. You even gave me clothes when I needed them. You may not have done any of this to me personally, but whenever you did something like that to a person in need, you did it to me!' To the bad people God will say, 'Get out of my sight. I don't want to have anything to do with you!'"

Jesus Eats His
Last Meal with His Friends

A few days later—in fact it was the Thursday before Jesus died—he rented a room so that he could celebrate the holy Passover meal with some of his very close friends. Peter, James and John were there. So were Andrew, Jude, and some other friends, including Judas. They ate all the special food that had been cooked for this feast, and they talked very solemnly about their ancestors being freed from slavery through God's help. They marveled how it seemed God always had a special love for them. They prayed some of their most holy prayers and even sang many of their favorite hymns.

Right after one of the prayers which they all said together, Jesus' friends noticed he was starting to do something very special to some of the bread on the table. He took the bread in his hands and prayed to God in heaven. Then he blessed the bread and said, "This is my body; take and eat it." Then he took a glass of wine and said, "Drink from this. This is a sign that we are sealing a new covenant of love and friendship. This is my blood." He drank from it and passed it around to his friends to drink. Everyone drank from the cup and then nobody said a word for the longest time. They were all praying with their eyes closed. While most of them were doing this Judas got up and slipped out.

Later on after they had started talking around the table again, for some reason or other a couple of Jesus' friends got into an argument at one end of the table about who was the

most important. Jesus stopped the argument by saying, "This is ridiculous! I don't think it's important at all whether any of you is the greatest or the best or the most powerful. I think what is important is whether you help and love other people. Are you willing to wait on people and do whatever is possible to help people in need? It is only when you are willing to help other people that you yourself become a really great person." After hearing these words, Jesus' friends were ashamed at the way they had been carrying on. Then to really make his point about helping people Jesus took a towel from one of the waiters and went around to all his friends in the room and washed their feet and hands in some water.

Jesus Prays
in the Park and Is Arrested

When the meal was finished they all went out into a nearby park and Jesus started to talk to them about some very serious things. He said, "The next couple of days are going to be pretty difficult for me. I'm going to need help from my friends to get through it all. But I'm a little worried because when things get going tough I think a lot of you are going to get frightened that you may lose your lives and not be around when I need you most."

The friends of Jesus all got a little uneasy because they

126

figured that what he said might be true. But Peter stood up and said, "Jesus, maybe you can't count on the rest of these guys to stick with you but you can count on me." Jesus laughed a little at what Peter said and then said, "Peter, I have a funny feeling that you'll be the first to scream 'I don't know him, he's not my friend' if a situation ever came up where you might be thrown in jail or hurt because you know me. In fact I'd be willing to bet that you will deny you know me at least three times in the next couple of days."

It was getting pretty late, but Jesus decided that he wanted to spend a little time thinking and praying before going to bed, so he took three of his friends to another section of the park. Jesus said to them: "I'm going over there for a while to pray by myself. Maybe you three could pray here together." It was very late at night by now, and Jesus' friends were very tired. They were so tired that instead of praying they all fell asleep, even though Jesus came over to them three times to try to wake them.

While Jesus was still praying, Judas came up to him. Judas had some policemen with him. (Judas had been a good friend of Jesus but then had turned against him.) When Jesus saw them coming he got up. Judas came over to Jesus and gave him a kiss on the cheek. (The kiss was a signal for the police to arrest Jesus.)

As they started to grab Jesus, Peter got very angry. He pulled out his sword and started to swing it at the people to scare them away. He ended up cutting off someone's ear before Jesus could say, "Peter, put your sword away. I don't want any violence." Then before the police arrested Jesus and dragged him off to court, he picked up the ear and put it back on the man's head where it belonged. Immediately the ear was healed and the man could hear out of that ear again.

Peter Follows While Jesus
Is Taken to Court
and Sentenced To Die

Peter followed them, and when they went into the courthouse Peter stayed outside waiting to see what would happen. A woman came up to Peter and looked at him. She thought she had seen him somewhere before. Then she remembered and said, "Aren't you a friend of the man Jesus whom they just took into court?" Peter was afraid, so he said, "I don't know what you're talking about!" She was sure that he was lying, but she dropped the matter.

Inside the courtroom the judge was asking Jesus all kinds of questions about his friends, his work, and where he lived. The judge couldn't find any crime that Jesus had committed, so he sent him to another court.

While Jesus was being taken to the other court some people said to Peter, "Are you sure you're not a friend of Jesus?" Peter shouted back, "No!" One of them said, "I'm sure you are his friend." Again Peter said, "No, I'm not!" At that very moment a rooster crowed.

When Jesus got to the next court, the judge's name was Pilate. After asking Jesus many questions, Pilate couldn't find anything wrong that he had done either. However, he was afraid to just let Jesus go, so he made a deal with his advisors. Pilate said: "We'll give the people a choice. They can decide for themselves whether they want to let Jesus go free or that prisoner Barabbas that we've got locked up in our jail." Pilate was sure they would ask to let Jesus go. He took the two of them out on the front steps of the courthouse and asked the people to vote. He was shocked when they all shouted, "Free Barabbas! Free Barabbas!"

Pilate decided to have Jesus beaten up to see if that would satisfy the people. But when he brought Jesus back out to show the people what he had done to him, they just kept chanting: "Kill him! Kill him! Kill him!" Pilate was afraid to stand up to the crowd, so he condemned Jesus to death and they dragged him away.

They Nail Jesus
to the Cross and He Dies

They made Jesus carry his own cross but he got so weak that he couldn't walk another step with it on his shoulders, so the soldiers made a man named Simon help Jesus carry it. By this time Jesus had fallen on the ground quite a few times. His clothes were all dirty and he was bleeding from some cuts on his face. A woman who was standing on the side of the road felt very sorry for Jesus, so she took a clean handkerchief and wiped his face clean. Jesus was so weak that all he could do was smile at her.

When they got to the place where they were going to crucify Jesus, they nailed him to a cross and stood around waiting for him to die. It was a very gloomy day. Many of Jesus' friends were there. They were all terribly frightened and in a state of shock. A couple of very close friends tried to comfort Jesus' mother as she stood crying at the foot of the cross. Even the weather seemed very gloomy that day. The clouds were large and very dark. The sun could hardly shine through them. The wind seemed unusually cold and harsh.

While Jesus was hanging on the cross they threw things at him and hit him with sticks and made fun of him. They said things such as: "If you are the Son of God, come down off the cross and save yourself."

After about three hours Jesus looked up to heaven and said, "Father, I can do no more!" Then his whole body went limp and he died.

When the soldiers were sure that Jesus was dead, they took him down and some friends buried him in a tomb which was in a nearby cemetery.

A Messenger of God Talks
to Some Women
Who Visits Jesus' Grave

Some armed guards were put in front of Jesus' grave because there was a rumor going around that some of Jesus' friends would try to steal his body from the grave. No one did try to steal his body, but the next Sunday a couple of women came to the cemetery to visit Jesus' grave. When they got near the grave there was a sudden earthquake. An angel came and opened the grave up. The angel's face was as bright as the sun. The guards were so frightened they actually froze and couldn't move. The angel spoke to the women. He said, "Don't be afraid. I'm a friend. You're looking for Jesus, aren't you? Well, he's not here. He has risen, just as he said he would. Take a look in the grave and then go and tell his friends."

John and Peter
Run to Jesus' Grave

When Peter and John heard that Jesus had risen from the dead they had to see this for themselves, so they started to run to the grave. When they reached the tomb, Peter went in first. He looked around the room but all he found were some clothes in which Jesus had been wrapped. They were placed neatly in a corner. This whole event made them believe that Jesus had truly risen.

Jesus Talks
to His Friend Mary

Later on, more of Jesus' friends came to the grave. After everyone left, one woman stayed around. Her name was Mary Magdalene, and she was crying. An angel said to her, "Why are you crying?" She answered: "Because someone has taken Jesus and I don't know where his body has been placed." As she was saying this she looked up and saw a man standing there. It was Jesus but she didn't recognize him. She said, "Where is he? Tell me so that I can take his body and have it buried." Jesus just said "Mary!" and she recognized him immediately. She ran toward him to embrace him, but he said, "No, Mary, don't touch me yet because I have not gone to my Father yet. Go now and tell the others that you have seen me and that I am alive."

Jesus Talks
to Two of His Friends

One day, when the news that Jesus had risen from the dead was still the main topic of every conversation, two of Jesus' friends were going out to dinner. Needless to say, they were talking together about the facts that Peter and John had given them concerning Jesus' being raised from the dead.

While they were walking along, a stranger who was walking in the same direction overheard some of their conversation.

(The stranger was actually Jesus but the two friends didn't recognize him.) He was curious to hear what they were saying, so he said, "Excuse me, but I couldn't help overhearing some of your conversation. What are you two so excited about?" The two friends told him all about the incredible but true story of Jesus from beginning to end. As the three of them walked along together, one thing led to another and the two friends invited the stranger to eat dinner with them.

When they were seated around a table, a waiter brought over a basket of bread. Jesus picked up the bread, blessed it and gave a piece to each of the two friends. When Jesus did this their mouths dropped open and they were speechless. Their faces turned bright red, because it was only after talking with him for about two hours that the two friends finally realized that they were talking to Jesus himself. They couldn't wait to tell Peter and John and their other friends all about meeting Jesus. In fact they were so excited that they didn't sleep a wink.

Jesus Visits
Peter and His Other Friends

The week after Jesus was killed his friends were still afraid of what might happen to them if they went out on the streets, so they locked themselves in a room. They wanted to hide out until people began to forget about Jesus. While they were hiding Jesus appeared to them.

He calmed their nerves by saying, "Peace to all of you." Then he talked to them for a while about different things. After they felt more relaxed he said to them: "You know that my Father in heaven sent me to do a job. I was to spread the message of God's love and salvation to all men, and now I want you to continue my work. I will send you the Holy Spirit who will give you the strength and courage and wisdom to preach this good news."

That day everyone was there to see Jesus except the apostle named Thomas. When the other apostles tried to tell Thomas

about seeing Jesus, he said, "I don't believe a word you're saying. You're making the whole thing up. I won't believe Jesus appeared to you until I see him with my own eyes and touch him with my own hands."

About a week later all of the apostles, including Thomas, were together when Jesus came to talk to them again.

He said, "Peace be with all of you." Then he turned to Thomas and said, "You see me, don't you? Come over here and touch me." Thomas was very frightened, but he answered: "My Lord and my God."

Looking at Thomas, Jesus said, "Thomas, you only believed in me after you saw me. There are going to be millions of people in the world who will believe in me even though they will never have the opportunity to see me as you have." Then Jesus left his friends.

Jesus Goes Back to His Father

A few days before Jesus was to leave, he made arrangements with his friends to meet him at noon on Thursday on the large hill in the park. He told them he had something very special to say to them. His friends were very curious and tried to figure out what he might be going to tell them.

When Thursday finally came, they met with Jesus, and he said, "This is the last time I'll see you all face to face. It's time for me to go back to my Father. What I'm going to tell you now is very important. I want you to go out into the world and tell everybody about God's love for them.

"Baptize them in the name of the Father and of the Son and of the Holy Spirit.

"Teach them everything I have taught you about living good lives. Anyone who believes what you say and is baptized will be saved.

"And remember, although you won't be able to see me, I'll be with you always!"

P.S. You might be interested to know, as I come to the end of writing this book, that everything I put in this book was put there to help you believe in Jesus and his way of life.